GW00750430

GALLERY OF
ANTIQUE ART

GALLERY OF
ANTIQUE ART

Paul Hetherington

RECENT
WORK
PRESS

Gallery of Antique Art
Recent Work Press
Canberra, Australia

Copyright © Paul Hetherington 2016

National Library of Australia
Cataloguing-in-Publication entry.

Hetherington, Paul

Gallery of Antique Art/ Paul Hetherington

ISBN: 9780994456540 (paperback)

A821.3

Cover illustration: 'Salle du Gladiateur'
reproduced under CreativeCommons Licence Attribution-ShareAlike 2.0
Cover design: Recent Work Press
Set in Palatino by Recent Work Press

recentworkpress.com

for Michelle

GALLERY MAP

First Room

There are no innocent tomorrows—Mary and child locked in their postures; a lanced Christ held in torsion on the cross. Possessing delicate colours of aftermath, the Annunciation astonishingly repeats. Christ's image is carried on a towel; Hypatia's skin is flayed with oyster shells. To leave is a parable; to stay home conjures apostasy or prayer. The statued Elect are white as a Pope's brittle frown. The Icon of Tenderness looks towards her feet.

Second Room

Yes, it is mainly about cruelty. Those sweet untouched Virgins dandling their Christ children—it's so powerful because unreal; how we all stupidly dream of our mothers taking us up. The painters knew that virgins were assaulted, children sold; how John foretold a crucified Christ. If we're unlucky, the image is every one of us—skewered by soldiers who happen to hold a lance. In the paintings they look subhuman, sin grinding bones and blood, but they are doing what they've been told—pushing gainsayers and refugees back. Seas in these paintings support many sails— and capture Christ's rebuke of the storm. We'd also unstorm the seas if we could, and unstory lies about the right and good.

Second Room (Perambulation)

For minutes at a time we stand in different postures,
trying them on for size. Anonymous men and women
look back with oddly captivating eyes, yet they do
not see us. In Caravaggio's rendering, John the
Baptist sits inside an abstract dream. Young though
he is, he might be considering Salome. As he does so,
lovers' portraits beguile old walls like a confusion of
memories. Hundreds of beautiful gazes and clothes.
The Etruscan *Sarcophogus of the Spouses* is delicate in
its reassembled terracotta. The figures look towards
eternity, reaching for vanished wine.

Third Room

We can choose not to believe it—pious grace and glory writ large on the walls. We can decide to accept beauty hanging close to where we stand. Exhausted, we're able to step into dirty streets and redolent decay. But near the door there's a seven-year-old girl dressed formally in green. Her gaze might be modern: hope, expectation, puzzlement—the painter's caught it well—and a sense of fractiousness as if she's sick of standing still.

Third Room (Perambulation)

The Virgin is attentive, holding her haloed child underneath a tree. The tree's cruciform languidly crawls with fruit like wounds and a spilled cup leaks water. If her gaze sees the future she won't observe it— what matters today is his vulnerable, pliable flesh. She quietens tremors that run through his wrists and feet as his eyes wander. Distant sunshine lights a garden where a man is being led, as if he's a figure in the child's innocent dream. She will bathe him as long as she can, in tears and soft shade.

INTERLUDE AND REFLECTION:
CAFÉ

Pietà

How crying is never done, his
body heavy in her hands. She has
dandled and rehearsed a thousand
deaths, and he won't reply to
her suffering. What she wears
she'll always wear—the blue of
implacable sorrow. It lies here as
unspeakable utterance.

Salome

*In Titian's depiction she is delicate
and distant, as if this head on a
platter was always her mother's
request. As if John the Baptist was
merely another preacher who'd
never persuaded her—after all,
there'd always been numerous gods.
Her mother had railed against him
and she understood why. His stern
injunctions hardly fitted the times.
And now he's far too heavy in her
hands—she has no wish to see him.*

Main Corridor

The meandering feeling in these corridors suggests there are too many depictions of the ideal—religious iconography supported by kneeling donors; courtly love; chivalric and civil grace. The poor are almost nowhere, performing bit parts in fields or as dark-faced executioners. Or they're an aside in someone else's conversation—servants who wait on the princely couple; witnesses to the righteous who have declined to ruin them. Fragility is the contrast between varnished gazes, damasked finery and the Baptist's severed head. Salome looks puzzled. What is it to stand in perpetuity proffering an image of the famous dead?

Fourth (Small) Room

If only, when we turned the corner, there were not more pictures. If only Caravaggio's young John the Baptist didn't look so knowing. If only the idea of baptism didn't make us think of dousing our heads, so hot it is and only eleven am. We discuss whether to continue, and we do, but now it's hard to pay attention to myriad Virgins or an eviscerated Prometheus. The eagle considers his guts like a form of meditation, and the liver looks ready to slide from the painting. Fire, water, the scorched earth of Crusades—so much inheres in sticky air. You point to paintings mimicking Callot's etchings of war—a burning monastery; a pillaged house; offenders hanging high; someone being broken on a wheel. Last rites are humidly murmured in the dying ear.

Fifth Room

In scholar-king Ashurbanipal's reign, Assyrian art was unsurpassed. Lion hunts, a garden party, glorious existence at fabled Ninevah in stone relief. And the storming of walls, flaying alive of prisoners: 'Susa, the great holy city, abode of their gods, seat of their mysteries, I conquered … I devastated the provinces of Elam and on their lands I sowed salt.' Corpses inhabit a river as if swimming in loss forever. The Elam King's head hangs in the garden. Lions fall under arrows. Ashurbanipal's cuneiform library held works on astronomy, mathematics and medicine, the Gilgamesh epic. A record of unimpeachable things.

Sixth (Back) Room

Indentations in the palazzo's stairs remember those who walked here—an aristocratic family who loved to fish and hunt. A brochure says this room was used for storing game—wild duck, pheasant, venison, all hung and brought to table. Now paintings line the walls, patching it with colour—paint that lifts away despite conservators' best efforts. Caravaggio's views of saintliness hold the wandering eye, his works twitching like live animals.

At a Window

The theme is always duration—humanity knowing
itself so persistently that nothing surprises. Paintings
trawl time like nets, catching what stories they can,
and ruins are the ground you walk. Dig up this gallery
and a palace lies beneath. The art reflects it—not only
ancient buildings' gravitas, but belief's reiteration. It's
as if the Agony in the Garden happened just last week,
and in the street there's Titian's young Adonis. Less
has changed than you think.

Seventh Room (Sculpture)

The Roman sculptures stand on newly polished plinths. Someone says 'art' and the word excites again, although we're standing among it like athletes surrounded by a team. The feeling connects with bouncing a football on grass. It was out of shape with split stitching. Across the oval's shifting space were lines of suburban streets, and the ball unsettled them. Here a corner of the room shows an ancient Adonis—whatever name he had then—made before Rome began. He rises from the year's sacrifice in shafts of brief light. There's something perfunctory and contained in his reaching torso—a wieldy simplicity like a ball thudding on turf.

INTERLUDE AND REFLECTION:
GALLERY GARDEN

Garden

We'd not understood the colour
green until we entered here—tender
and wet, like a honeydew melon
so ripe that scent washes the flesh.
We weren't fully connected until
we walked under a night sky and
read its old cuneiform, dazzled into
a gathering exuberance. We'd not
felt love as a moving image until we
stood before a thousand paintings
in a day and, turning to each other,
saw intimacies rise like tender
newsreels.

Eve

As the sculpture points her finger
you know you're being addressed.
You lean closer and her lips frame
a frozen verb, intricate secrecies
veined in her glance. She's Eve in
the Garden as Adam turns away.
Lost knowledge marbles her mouth.

Saint Agatha

*She carries her globed innocence
with the knowledge that it won't
protect her. She knows pain as a
shearing of self but holds herself
upright. Though obliteration will
come, yet the garden's scents
remain. She sees reds and yellows
on stems and the delicacy sustains
her—bird song, insects' flight. What
her belief promises is elusive as
sunset, purpling each day's end.
She waits to be tipped into haloed
saturation.*

Statues

Rooms possessed us, their statues walking with hundreds of stiff-gaited farewells. History gathered us into Penelope's loom: teased out, threaded, unpicked. Boots, armour, drawn swords—we were marched towards absence next to broken arms, fractured torsos, lost noses. Obliteration gazed with a hundred blank eyes.

History

*An aqueduct strides across the
landscape in broken steps and the
train rocks. History catches you; old
bricks lean towards the carriage,
water reaches from a damaged
channel like a multi-armed god.
You see yellow and green light; a
stretching meadow; a few scrappy
trees. Earth tips from an exposed
bank and a man lays his jacket on
a broken arcade. A tunnel swallows
you like piped water.*

Eighth Room (Special Exhibition of Dutch Paintings)

When you stumble on flagstones I seize your arm.
We climb marble steps, feeling their old weight in
our legs. As we enter, there are a hundred crowded
Dutch paintings showing seventeenth-century fruit
and meat. The ticket seller's playing Bach's inimitable
Cello Suites, but the sound's so low I query what it
is. The largo speaks of Spain, where we listened and
were entranced; where we sat on a balcony as you
offered counsel. I'm reminded that affection's often like
this—a helping hand, music no-one expects. Someone
says right words and the aftermath enthralls—like a
painting one could eat.

Ninth Room

How artists' hands have travelled and known
uncountenanced worlds—and here are pickings
from improbable treasures. Looted jewellery, hoards
of coin, necklaces carved from ivory. Yet none's as
valuable as this small portrait that understands light's
scrupulousness. We imagine this: a man holds a candle
as his master paints past midnight. Goblets of wine
gather winks. We shift feet, looking at the rendition
of lace they made; looking at the painting's frown.
The concentration's both inward and outward. We are
absorbed in her meticulous, exotic gown.

Ninth Room (Perambulation)

I'm standing quietly and a painting speaks—of how
there were floods for nearly a week and not far from
here the Tiber rose. But, after all, a tour's arrived and
a guide's instructing her group: 'It's neat how he's
painted her feet.' They move on and I examine again
the Virgin with crucified child. Desert sun bakes the
blue of her grief—it's almost all she knows. And
grace she carries; divinity that dies; the world's long
heaviness. She'd hold him forever if time would stand
still. She'd let him go if she could.

Tenth Room

There's a painting of a dark-haired saint caught by a hateful crowd. And an agonised Prometheus clinging to his rock like a falling climber. Two tax collectors sit with glinting coins under a sixteenth century window; someone else is slitting another's throat. Yet, turning a corner, this painting is my daughter, with blonde hair and familiar gaze. 'What are you doing here?' I say aloud. A smile hovers at the corner of her mouth; her young wisdom brightens a small boudoir. I stand for an hour, immersed in her kindliness. She's finely dressed, dated 1753.

Tenth Room (Perambulation)

Believing in this past is no longer possible. Not with
so many depictions of Saint Catherine's broken wheel
or the painterly zeal of righteous crusades—the meek
inheriting loss's deep umber. It's a visual hagiography
writ large, that afterwards our dreams irritatingly
repeat. Yet Giorgione's tempest makes of today's
storm an urgent poiesis and parable and the suffering
Madonna strangely understands contemporary grief.
Everywhere we look—implausible lies, improbable
truth.

INTERLUDE AND REFLECTION:
GALLERY SHOP

Postcard: Santa Maria del Popolo

*In Santa Maria del Popolo Saul
is gasping on his back. Words
enter his body like creatures;
he embraces his interrogator in
armfuls of puzzled air. Belief,
knowledge, trust collide as light
is taken from his eyes. His groom
looks on uncertainly; his horse
steps forwards, exiting the frame.
Caravaggio suggests there's no way
back from such extremity—which
his crucified Saint Peter underlines.
'Beware of what you know,' the
paintings say.*

Postcard:
Capuchin
Crypt

*The crypt is a delicacy of design;
air remembers blood that lodged
here. Shrugged dances of shoulder
blades are Angels ceaselessly trying
ascent. Rooms are full of smiles,
each one a death's head. Sing
they say. Drive to eternal love via
bony congregations. Take a hand
that aggregates phalanges and
metacarpals; feel its broken hold,
leading into byways of knowledge;
enshrinements of the body's first
geography. That bay of the skull;
this coastline of rib. These bones
stood up, fixed by intention. Now
they are white noise.*

Book:
Herculaneum

*The old town is a first-century
fisherman's sudden nightmare—
beautiful light, yellowing ruins;
broken frescoes like licentious
glimpses. Mosaics are milky
memories dropped willy-nilly on
floors. It's a husk without kernel;
a vast decision's inarticulate
aftermath. Hot yellows and reds
remain as if a boudoir's light has
been written a hundred times in
open air. Cooking pots, toilets,
plumbing are a catalogue of
absent domestic intimacies. And a
thousand burnt papyri are balled
in a library. Read with x-rays,
they speak black recollections of
days before loss. When the pagan
world stood prosperously beneath
conflagration.*

Book:
Pompeii

Pompeii is forgetfulness. Shrines
with no ceremonies to garland
them; piazzas without throngs;
ovens without bread. Brothels
are frankly frescoed but years of
anticipatory waiting have dissolved
into earth. Painters inhabit fragile
works, rubbed by backpacks of
tourists, and makers of mosaics
have long since given up abraded
delicacies of their hands. So many
patterns to left and right of straight-
lined streets; so much candour
in buildings without roofs—air
tunnels through bedroom, atrium,
hortus alike; alien words rebound
from buildings. What's left are
intricate structures of mind. Follow
them and find yourself lost on
rutted stone. Hear shouts of the
future, heavy as raining pumice,
overlaying your life.

Gift Card: St Peter's

In St. Peter's the space is an eddy of design. Sculptures lean like teachers giving lessons; angels are ascending but never quite out of view. Vastness reaches towards us. I imagine my dead friend floating there, almost angelic in his winged quest for flight. It's like a blasphemy—so much gravitas surrounds us—yet I'm sure he's near, preaching his own ideas of good and right. It's long and digressive, rambling like this wide air. There's something true in the thought—that he's finding a way of believing.

Eleventh Room (Small Annex)

A twelfth century scroll shows *The Tale of Genji* in aristocratic red and gold—and green 'like sea grass steeped in brine'. Outside in a Japanese Garden a thousand watery fingers are tapping on stone, as if counting centuries. Congregating koi are bundled scarves; autumn leaves spread like brocade. Genji's thoughts are constellating pines and a sleeved river's foam. At Nijo the Lady of the Orange Blossoms has moved into the east lodge. Genji remembers the speech of Akashi fishermen, as incomprehensible as birds.

Twelfth Room (Italian Portraits)

Wearing brilliant fineries, the portraits look at us like interlopers. This young woman in intricate sleeves believes in the rights of pope and aristocracy—after all, they are her family. She understands implicit nuances of style. Her husband stares with wary and uncivil gaze. Facing them is a *Martyrdom of St Matthew*. They assess his pain implacably, and the raised executioner's knife.

Courtyard

The palazzo's wide corridors and rooms breathe
various shapes: columns, stairs, arches—so many
hours to sculpt a building. The courtyard's original
Renaissance fountain gargles next to old gods. The
sculptures are mostly Roman copies and confections of
pillaged fragments—ancient fakes that resemble only
themselves. There's no going back; no resumption of
abandoned beauty. The fabric of a rare Greek original
is sinuous water on fractured stone.

Hallway

We're ensconced in the tenebrous corridors and hallways, travelling steadily from image to image. Servants in this old palazzo have long since washed blood from walls; its distant cellars are conspicuously quiet. History's in a mouse's transgressions; and the sidling manners of the breeze. Like expensive wallpaper, pictures beautifully cover the walls. A famous painter noted pragmatic cruelty hovering at the corners of a Pope's closed mouth, as taxes from brothels gilded the picture frames.

Thirteenth Room (Spanish Paintings)

Spanish paintings know the marriage of cruelty and misericordia—black sadness, as if oil and varnish are a congealed lamentation. The lanced Christ twists while the Agony in the Garden is reinscribed throughout the Americas. Smallpox blisters are bulging, uncryable tears. As the Spanish hung heathens from their masts and burnt the Mayan books; as they preached God's charity and recorded their conquests, their fires disarticulated uncountable years.

Fourteenth Room

We are framed and jostled by paintings that won't leave
us alone—everywhere we walk, every conversation.
The way we see each other draws from these gazes,
and still the raddled saints' relentless pieties disturb.
None of the aristocrats look like anyone we'd ever
want to know. You're suddenly formal, as if a minor
noble is escorting us and I fall into step. We whisper
about rooms—furniture that amazes, silk on walls,
extraordinary gestures of marble and plaster. No law
courts would contradict such grandeur. My neck feels
exposed.

Fifteenth Room (Renaissance Religious Paintings)

There is never enough time to understand the art. Images seem to liquefy; pictures of saints infect sunlight. It's as if grace was long ago dropped nearby and we can't pick it up. The weight of this seeing connotes innumerable centuries. Yet the Madonna on the left shows simple humility and a young man facing his future looks humane. He offers a teetering chalice.

Sixteenth Room (Etruscan Remains)

The Etruscans are known in shards and sculptures, fragments of writing and pieces of building. And for trading in marvellous Greek amphorae; a dedication to a lost religion. The Romans were taught in their civilised cities before returning to ruin them, planting phalluses on sacred ground. We see populous remains, like footprints on friable earth; or a jumble of leavings someone picked up. We have learnt to revere them but they don't speak back. They're a dial whose time is jammed, believing in beauty we cannot create. They search us with eyes that are incurably blind.

INTERLUDE AND REFLECTION:
LEAVING THE GALLERY

Storm

for AC

Like heavy eyes, shutters on shops
are pulled. Days and years like
this, as money enters and leaves
a till. Birds make a mess of the
square, lights in museums flicker.
Giorgione's La Tempesta *glows*
where portable air conditioners
fail to cool the rooms. The enigma
is not art itself, but why standing
here's a comfort as Europe's
bourses crash. Insects are chewing
backs of canvases; old Italian
illusions dissolve. Giorgione's paint
luminesces—a city, a storm, a
woman, a child, a man ...

Blackouts

for CE

The blackouts are unreasonably persistent. Paintings darken on our walls. The old Madonna you bought is crying silvered tears. Tomato sauce bubbles in a pan and you stir while pointing to the skyline's smears of fire and candleflame. Soon the city will resume its business in electric light but we are already dispossessed. We've passed through so many doors, and climbed so many dark stairways to museums. You were avid, standing near surreal halos and thick impastos of grace. Your eye shifted towards new rooms and corridors. And, in the first blackout, as we huddled near one of Caravaggio's saints, you pointed to a man in an overcoat. 'Who is he?' you gestured as he stepped left and out of sight.

Acknowledgements

I would like to thank the various people who shared my journey in writing these prose poems. Their contributions and interventions were often crucial. I gratefully acknowledge the award of a six-month Australia Council for the Arts Residency in the BR Whiting Studio in Rome during 2015-16, where these poems were written. I am indebted to Cassandra Atherton, Adrian Caesar and Paul Munden for editing the manuscript so astutely. And I thank Shane Strange of Recent Work Press for suggesting their publication.

Australian Government

Australia Council for the Arts

Illustrations

(reproduced under Creative Commons Licence Attribution-ShareAlike 2.0) pg.6 'Art Gallery of NSW interior' (detail); pg.12 'Up we go' [modified] by Bat in the rain, 2008; pg.16 'palazzo nuovo gallery' [modified] by xuan che, 2010; pg.29 'Le portique peint de la Villa Giulia (Rome)' [modified] by Jean-Pierre Dalbéra, 2011; pg.43 'Sant'Agnese in Agone - Rome, Piazza Navona' by Roma Opera Omnia; pg.52 'Le portique du palais Barberini' [modified] by Jean-Pierre Dalbéra, 2011.

Paul Hetherington is Professor of Writing in the Faculty of Arts and Design at the University of Canberra and Head of the International Poetry Studies Institute (IPSI) there. He has published ten previous books of poetry and five chapbooks. He has an abiding interest in the visual arts and edited the final three volumes of the National Library of Australia's four-volume edition of the diaries of the artist Donald Friend. He is one of the founding editors of the international online journal *Axon: Creative Explorations* and a founding editorial committee member of the *Meniscus* journal. He won the 2014 Western Australian Premier's Book Awards (poetry) and was awarded a six-month Australia Council for the Arts Residency in the BR Whiting Studio in Rome for 2015-16. He was also awarded one of the two places on the 2012 Australian Poetry Tour to Ireland and shortlisted for the 2013 Montreal International Poetry Prize. He was shortlisted for and commended in the 2016 Newcastle Poetry Prize.

More Recent Work

Owen Bullock	*Urban Haiku (2015)* *River's Edge (2016)*
Paul Hetherington	*Gallery of Antique Art (2016)*
Niloofar Fanaiyan	*Transit (2016)*
Prose Poetry Project	*Seam (2015)* *Pulse (2016)*
Jen Webb	*Sentences from the Archive (2016)*
Monica Carroll, Jen Crawford, Owen Bullock & Shane Strange	*5 6 7 8 (2016)*
Subhash Jaireth	*Incantations (2016)*

all titles available from
recentworkpress.com

RECENT
WORK
PRESS

www.ingramcontent.com/pod-product-compliance
Ingram Content Group UK Ltd.
Pitfield, Milton Keynes, MK11 3LW, UK
UKHW040633040225
4435UKWH00033B/394